EVERYDAY INVENTIONS

On the Move

Jane Bidder

W

FRANKLIN WATTS
LONDON•SYDNEY

First published in 2006 by
Franklin Watts
338 Euston Road
London NW1 3BH

Franklin Watts Australia
Hachette Children's Books
Level 17/207 Kent Street
Sydney NSW 2000

Series editor: Jennifer Schofield
Designer: Ross George
Picture researcher: Diana Morris
Artwork: Anthony Cutting

Acknowledgements:
The author would like to thank Marry Bellis
of http://inventors.about.com for her help
in researching this book.
AKG Images: 18b. Cody Images: 16t. Mary Evans
Picture Library; 6b, 9b, 10b, 12t, 12b, 13, 14, 16b,
19, 21, 22b, 24b. Chris Fairclough/Watts: 10t. Ford
Motor Company: 4b. National Museum of Roller
Skating, Lincoln, Nebraska, USA: 23. Parry/Topham:
25c. Photonews/Topham: 25b. Photri/Topham: 24.
Topham: 4t, 7b, 8t, 8b, 11, 15, 17, 18t, 20, 24t, 25.
James Witham/Team Suzuki: 3b, 14t.

A CIP catalogue record for this book
is available from the British Library.

ISBN: 0 7946 6402 9
Dewey Classification: 609

Printed in China

Contents

About inventions

An invention is a device or gadget that is designed and made for the first time. The person who makes the device is called an inventor. In this book, we look at inventions that help people to move about, who invented them and how they have changed over time.

Making life easier

Many types of transport have been invented because people want to improve their lives. For example, it is much easier to go by bus than to spend hours walking from place to place. Not only do inventions like buses make our lives easier by saving us time, but they have also changed the way we live.

Linked to each other

Many forms of transport have relied on one major breakthrough leading to changes elsewhere. For example, few inventions in this book would have happened without the invention of the wheel about 6,000 years ago.

Developing ideas

Not all inventions are thought of instantly - many of them are changed and improved over time. For example, the first motorbikes looked like bicycles with steam-powered engines. The engines were not very practical and soon they were replaced by petrol-powered engines. Today, not all motorbikes run on petrol - some run on electricity.

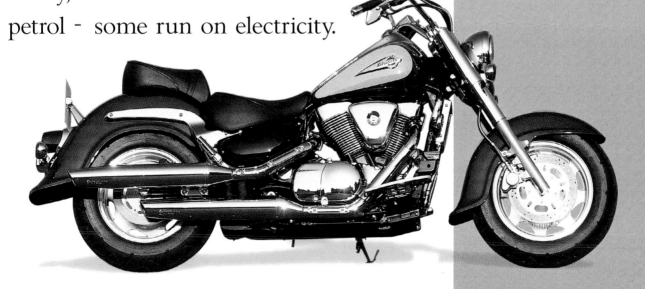

TIMELINES

You will find timelines throughout this book. They show in date order when a specific breakthrough or invention occurred.

Sometimes the dates are very exact, but other times they point to a particular decade (period of ten years), for example the 1920s.

Use these timelines to keep track of when things happened.

Cars

Today's cars have four wheels, and an engine that runs on petrol or diesel. They are made of metal and built for safety and comfort, with safety belts, airbags and padded seats. But cars were not always like this. The first car did not travel very fast and was built mainly from wood.

How does a car work?
A car's engine burns petrol or diesel and uses the energy this creates to turn the wheels.

The Fardier

The very first car was invented in 1769 and was called the Fardier. It had three wheels and was powered by steam. It could carry only two people and its top speed was just over 6 km/h.

Petrol power

The first car powered by petrol was probably built in 1889 by Gottlieb Daimler and Wilhelm Mayback. It was faster than the Fardier and could travel up to 16 km/h.

Fabulous Fords

A big breakthrough came in 1908 when Henry Ford's factory produced the Model T car. Over the next 19 years his company made more than 18 million cars. Ford still makes cars that are sold all over the world.

TIMELINE

1769
Frenchman Nicholas-Joseph Cugnot makes the Fardier.

1889
The first petrol-driven car is built in Germany by Gottlieb Daimler and Wilhelm Mayback.

1908
The American Henry Ford produces the first Model T Ford.

1930s
Adolf Hitler asks Dr Ferdinand Porche to produce a cheap car for the German people. By 1938, the first Volkswagen Beetles are on the road.

1946
Rover makes the first gas turbine-powered motorcar.

1997
The Toyota Prius is sold in Japan. It is a hybrid car that runs on a mixture of petrol and electricity.

Bicycles

You may already know how to ride a bicycle or you may be learning how to turn the pedals. But did you know that the first bicycle had no pedals?

Foot power

The very first bicycle was known as the 'celeripede'. It had no pedals, gears or even a chain - you just sat on it and pushed it along with your feet.

Bone shakers

In 1861, Pierre Michaux fixed cranks, like pedals, onto the front wheels of the celeripede and called it a 'velocipede'. It was also known as a 'bone shaker', because your whole body shook when you rode it!

Rovers

The big break for bicycles came in 1895 when James Starley from England made the Rover. The Rover's pedals turned a gear wheel, which was linked to the back wheel by a chain. Like today's bicycles, the Rover's chain went around with the pedals, turning the wheels. The Rover was also known as the Safety Bicycle.

1816
The celeripede is designed by the Frenchman J Niepce.

1861
France's Pierre Michaux makes the 'bone shaker'.

1870s
The Penny Farthing is invented – it has a large front wheel and a small back wheel.

1895
James Starley designs the Rover.

1930s
Bicycles now have rubber tyres and are easier to ride.

1940s
Tandem bicycles, with one bike joined to another, are invented.

1977
America's Joe Breeze builds a mountain bike, called Breezer No. 1. Only ten bikes are made, but the craze soon catches on.

Trains

In many countries around the world, trains are a fast and inexpensive way to travel. It is hard to imagine that the very first trains were carts pulled along rails by horses.

The Rocket

In 1829, George Stephenson from England built a new steam engine called the Rocket. It could pull a train for 56 km in less than two hours.

Railroads in the USA

Before trains ran across the USA, many western states were hard to reach. In the 1860s, two companies, the Central Pacific Railroad from California and the Union Pacific Railroad from New York, set out to build tracks across the USA. In 1869, a spike was put in the ground in Utah to mark where the two companies met.

Terrific TGVs

The TGV is France's high-speed train. TGVs and trains developed from the TGV run in countries around the world - for example in the USA, the Netherlands and South Korea. In 2003, a TGV travelling in England reached an amazing speed of 334.7 km/h.

TIMELINE

1804
England's Richard Trevithick builds the first steam engine.

1824
The first public railway opens in England, between Stockton and Darlington.

1829
George Stephenson makes the Rocket.

1830
The first public railroad is built in the USA, linking Baltimore and Ohio.

1920s
Electric and diesel trains begin to replace steam trains.

1964
A 'bullet' train is built in Japan; it can travel at more than 200 km/h.

1981
France's first TGV service runs from Paris to Lyon.

Buses

All over the world, buses cover great distances. In England's capital, London, each bus travels up to 1.2 million kilometres in its lifetime - that is the same as travelling to the Moon and back!

Paris Vécu. — Une Station d'Omnibus   L J & Cie, éd

Horse-power

Paris was the first city to use buses. The French buses were nothing like the buses of today - they were pulled by horses.

Steam engines

In 1829, a steam-engined coach was designed in Britain. Although these coaches travelled faster than horse-drawn buses, not many were made because drivers had to pay a fee for using them on the roads.

Just like cars

In about 1919, when car engines were being developed, steam buses were replaced by petrol-run buses. A year later, in 1920, buses were also designed with covered tops and rubber tyres to make them more comfortable.

TIMELINE

1672
Buses are pulled by horses in Paris.

1829
England's George Shillibeer runs the first bus service in London.

1829
Sir Goldworthy Gurney of Britain makes the first steam-engined bus.

1904
Sight-seeing buses are used in the USA.

1914
Greyhound buses begin taking passengers from city to city in the USA.

1919
Petrol buses are used.

1920
Buses with covered roofs and rubber tyres are made.

Motorbikes

Some motorbikes can travel at incredible speeds of over 200 km/h, so it is hard to imagine that some of the early bikes travelled at speeds of only about 11km/h.

Howard-Roper's motorbike

In 1869, America's Sylvester Howard-Roper made a steam-engined motorbike. It was not very practical as its engine constantly needed topping up with coal.

The father of the motorbike

In 1885, the German engineer Gottlieb Daimler fitted a small petrol engine onto a wooden bicycle frame. He is sometimes called 'the father of the motorbike'.

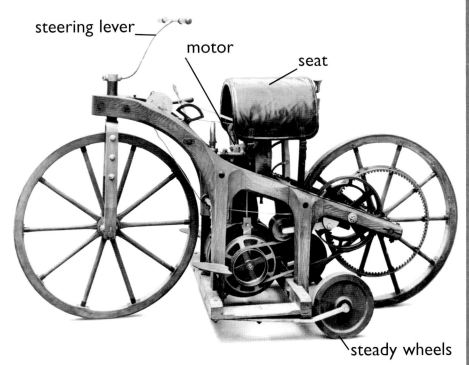

steering lever

motor

seat

steady wheels

Harley Davidsons

The Harley Davidson Motor Company was founded in 1903 by William Harley and Arthur and Walter Davidson. They started racing their bikes in 1914 and became known as the 'Wrecking Crew' because they won so often.

TIMELINE

1869
The American Sylvester Howard-Roper designs the first steam motorbike.

1884
England's Edward Butler puts a petrol engine on a tricycle.

1885
Gottlieb Daimler fits a petrol engine on to a bicycle frame.

1894
Germany's Hildebrand and Wolfmueller make the first production motorbike.

1903
The Harley Davidson Motor Company is formed in the USA and develops its first motorbike.

2005
The American company eCycle begins testing a hybrid motorbike, that runs on electricity.

Aeroplanes

Inventors had been trying to make flying machines from as early as 400

BCE, when the Greek Archytas is said to have built a wooden pigeon that moved through the air with steam. Since then, flying machines have come a long way.

Flying around!

In 1903, the American brothers Wilbur and Orville Wright invented the first aeroplane. Their first flight lasted only 12 seconds.

Brilliant Boeings

In 1969, the first Boeing 747 (see left) was built. At the time, the 747 was the largest passenger aeroplane - its tail alone was taller than a six-storey building! The first 747 could carry 400 people and could fly at more than 1,000 km/h. Many of today's planes are updated versions of the 747.

Concorde

Concorde was the world's first passenger aeroplane to travel faster than the speed of sound. These supersonic planes were used for passengers from 1976. However, in 2003 they were taken out of service.

TIMELINE

1903
The Wright brothers fly the first aeroplane.

1909
The Frenchman Louis Bleriot flies across the English Channel in his Bleriot XI monoplane.

1930
Amy Johnson flies from England to Australia.

1937
Germany's Hans von Ohain builds the first jet engine, the He178.

1960
The Hawker P1127 is able to make vertical take-offs and landings.

1969
The Boeing 747 is built.

1976
Concorde carries passengers for the first time.

2005
A new plane, the A380, is flown. It can carry more than 550 people.

Wheelchairs

We know a type of wheelchair was used as long ago as 530 BCE. Since then, wheelchairs have come a long way – from those that fold up to the lightweight three-wheeled models that athletes use.

Farfler's wheel chair

In 1655 Stephen Farfler, a paraplegic (someone who is not able to use his legs), designed his own wheelchair. It enabled him to move himself about using his arms, rather than relying on someone to push him.

Paralympics
The first Olympic-style games for disabled athletes were held in 1960. Today, the Paralympic Games include basketball, athletics and tennis for wheelchair athletes.

Bath chairs

In 1783, John Dawson from Bath in England developed the Bath chair. It looked like a large reclining chair with two big wheels at the back and one or two small wheels at the front.

Folding chairs

In 1933, the American Herbert A Everest wanted a wheelchair that he could get in and out of a car. He asked the English engineer HC Jennings to make a folding wheelchair. The wheelchair was a great success and modern folding wheelchairs are based on this design.

TIMELINE

530 BCE
The first type of wheelchair is shown on a Greek vase.

1595
A special 'invalid's chair' is built for Spain's King Philip II.

1655
Stephen Farfler designs his own wheelchair.

1783
The Bath chair is made in England.

1912
The first electric wheelchair is made.

1933
A folding wheelchair is made by England's HC Jennings.

1948
The first sporting event for wheelchair users is held in England.

Motorscooters

Sometimes one invention leads to another. For example, scooters were developed after motorbikes were made so that people had a cheaper way to get around.

The Autoped

It is unclear who invented the first motorscooter. However, some reports claim that the first one was called the Autoped. It had no seat, so the rider had to stand and move the steering column. Early scooters could travel at 16 km/h.

Parascooting!
During the Second World War, armies used parachutes to drop scooters near their troops so that they could move about.

The wasp

Soon after the Second World War, the Piaggio aeroplane factory developed a new scooter. When its owner, Enrico Piaggio heard the scooter, he exclaimed, 'Sembra una vespa' ('It's like a wasp') and the name Vespa stuck.

Lambretta scooters

The first Lambretta was made in 1947 to fill the need for cheap transport in Italy. It had a second seat (see above), making it able to carry passengers.

TIMELINE

1915
The Autoped is made in America.

1919
England's Granville Bradshaw makes the ABC Scootmota.

1920
Motorscooters become fashionable for men and women.

1940s
Scooters are used by armies during the Second World War.

1946
The first Vespas are made in Italy.

1947
Ferdinando Innocenti's company makes the first Lambretta.

Roller skates

Just as scooters followed on from the invention of the motorbike, so roller skates were developed from ice skates.

Roll away

The first roller skate was invented by Belgium's Jean-Joseph Merlin in 1760. Merlin would skate and play the violin at the same time, as a party trick.

However, Merlin had not found a way to stop suddenly, and one day he collided with a large mirror, injuring himself.

Get your skates on!

During the 1860s, James L Plimpton designed a roller skate with two pairs

of wheels on the heel and toe. He also opened his own skating rink.

Later, in the 1880s, the Americans Richardson and Raymond improved on skates' wheels by adding ball bearings, which made the skates go faster and more smoothly.

Ball bearings
Ball bearings are tiny steel balls that fit between a wheel and an axle. They keep the wheel moving smoothly.

Much lighter

During the 1940s, roller skates were designed with plastic wheels instead of metal, to make them lighter on the feet. They also had toe-stops for braking.

TIMELINE

1760
Merlin designs a boot for roller skating.

1860s
James Plimpton from America makes a better roller skate and opens a rink.

1880s
Richardson and Raymond make skates with ball bearings.

1940s
Roller skates are made from plastic to make them lighter and easier to skate in.

1989
America's Scott and Brennan Olson start a company to make a new kind of roller skate, called roller blades.

1990s
Skates are made from titanium to make them even lighter.

Helicopters

Helicopters are amazing flying machines. Their blades turn really fast to make them move, and because they do not need runways like aeroplanes do, they can take off and land in small spaces.

First flight

The first helicopter is said to have been invented in 1907 by a Frenchman called Paul Cornu. However, it flew for only a few seconds. As with many inventions, it took many other people to work on helicopters before they really took off!

Sikorsky's success

One of the most successful helicopter designers was Russia's Igor Sikorsky. He started designing helicopters in 1910. After many designers tried to build helicopters, Sikorsky finally designed the VS-300 in 1940. The VS-300 was used as a model for other helicopters and, as a result, Sikorsky is known as the 'father' of helicopters.

Helicopter power!
In 1986, a Westland Lynx is said to have flown at the amazing speed of 402 km/h.

Westland Lynx

In 1971, the Westland Lynx helicopter flew for the first time. Today, countries such as Denmark, Britain and France still use the Westland Lynx as a military helicopter.

TIMELINE

1907
France's Paul Cornu invents the first helicopter.

1910
Igor Sikorsky starts designing helicopters.

1924
France's Etienne Oehmichen flies a helicopter for 1 kilometre.

1940
The VS-300 is designed by Igor Sikorsky.

1971
The first Westland Lynx is made.

More inventions

Every day, people use many other forms of transport, too. For example, children are pushed in baby buggies or pushchairs to get them from place to place and many people use boats or ferries to travel to work or to go on holiday.

Baby buggies

It is difficult for young children to get about - especially if they are too small to walk. The first baby buggy was designed by England's William Kent in 1733. However, the big breakthrough in baby buggies came in 1965 when Owen Maclaren made the first folding buggy.

Ferries

Boats have been used to to ferry people across water for thousands of years. The first steam-powered ferry crossing of the English Channel is thought to have been in 1820. Today, ferries are used all over the world, transporting peope, cars and even trucks.

Pushscooters

Children's scooters have been around for about 100 years. In the early 2000s, folding metal scooters were made and they became popular with both children and adults.

RUBBER TYRES

Many inventions that help us to travel from place to place have wheels. Although the wheel has been around since prehistoric times, the rubber tyre used on many of the forms of transport is quite a new invention.

In 1888, John Boyd Dunlop had the idea of trapping air inside a rubber tyre after watching his son riding a bicycle with solid rubber tyres.

Then in 1895, the first air-filled car tyre was invented by the Michelin brothers. They showed off their new tyres on a car called Eclair.

Since the Michelin brothers' tyres, tyre manufacturers have developed tyres for different vehicles, such as trucks, tractors and aeroplanes.

Timeline

530 BCE

Wheelchairs are used – they look like beds on wheels.

1655

Stephen Farfler designs his own wheelchair.

1672

The first bus is invented.

1760

Jean-Joseph Merlin designs a boot for roller skating.

1769

The first steam-powered car is made by Nicholas Cugnot.

1804

Richard Trevithick invents the first steam train.

1816

The first bicycle is invented.

1860s

James Plimpton adds more wheels to roller skates.

1869

The first motorbike is made by Sylvester Howard-Roper.

1889

A petrol-driven car is built by Daimler and Mayback.

1903

The first aeroplane is made by the Wright brothers.

1907

Paul Cornu invents the first helicopter.

1908

Henry Ford makes a Model T car.

1915

The Autoped motorscooter is made.

1920

Buses with covered roofs and rubber tyres are made.

1933

A folding wheelchair is made.

1938

The first Volkswagen Beetles are on the road.

1946

The first Vespas are made in Italy.

1964

A 'bullet' train is built in Japan.

1968

The Boeing 747 is built.

1976

Concorde carries passengers for the first time.

1981

France's first TGV service runs from Paris to Lyon.

1997

The Toyota Prius, a hybrid car, is sold in Japan.

2005

The A380 aeroplane is flown for the first time.

Glossary

Axle
The pin or rod found in the centre of the wheel. The wheel turns around the axle.

Coal
A natural, brown or black hard substance that is burnt as a fuel.

Hitler, Adolf (1889–1945)
The German ruler during the Second World War.

Hybrid
A car or motorbike that is developed from other cars and motorbikes.

Invalid
Someone who has a long term illness or disability.

Paraplegic
Someone who cannot move the lower part of his or her body and often needs to use a wheelchair.

Prehistoric
From a time long before history was recorded.

Public
For everyone's use.

Railroad
A track laid with rails so that the wheels of a train can run on it.

Steady wheels
Smaller wheels that are attached to the back wheels of bicycles and motorbikes to keep the bike upright and steady.

Steering column
The pole found on a bicycle, car or motorbike that the steering wheel is attached to. The steering wheel is used to change direction.

Solo
Alone.

Supersonic
Faster than the speed of sound.

Titanium
A shiny white metal that is found in rocks. It is lightweight, strong and does not rust easily.

Websites

**www.nationalgeographic.com/
features/96/inventions/**
Have loads of fun playing games about
inventions.

www.howstuffworks.com
Find out how everyday inventions
work by searching for them on this
website.

**www.cybersteering.com/trimain/
history/ecars.html**
Follow the development and history
of the car, from its early days to
today's speed machines.

www.pedalinghistory.com
Find out everything there is to know
about bicycles from who invented
them to how they work.

**www.bbc.co.uk/schools/
famouspeople**
Click on George Stephenson to learn
all about the steam engine and how
he developed it.

**http://kids.discovery.com/
convergence/wright/wright.html**
Follow America's Wright brothers,
Wilbur and Orville, as they build their
first aeroplane and take off!

**www.sciencemuseum.org.uk/on-
line/flights/index.asp**
Go on a virtual tour of the British
Science Museum and follow the
development of famous inventions.

www.rollerskatingmuseum.com
Tour a roller-skating museum.

Note to parents:

Every effort has been made by the publishers to
ensure that the websites in this book are suitable
for children, that they are of the highest
educational value, and that they contain no
inappropriate or offensive material. However, due
to the nature of the Internet, it is impossible to
guarantee that the contents of these sites will not
be altered. We strongly advise that Internet access
is supervised by a responsible adult.

Index